# HISTORY OF BOSTON TEA PARTY

## A BRIEF OVERVIEW FROM BEGINNING TO END

### HISTORY ENCOUNTERS

# History of

# Boston Tea Party

## A Brief History from Beginning to the End

## History Encounters

authorized, approved, licensed, or endorsed by the original

book's author or publisher and any of their licensees or affiliates.

# CONTENTS

# Chapter One

# Introduction

On December 16, 1773, in Boston, Massachusetts, the Sons of Liberty staged a political and commercial protest known as the Boston Tea Party. At issue were the Townshend Acts, which required the British East India Company to collect taxes from American colonists before they could import Chinese tea for resale, and the Tea Act of May 10, 1773, which permitted the company to sell the tea without collecting any more taxes. They saw the Townshend Acts taxes as an infringement on their freedom; thus, the Sons of Liberty fought hard against them. Protesters burned a whole cargo of tea from the East India Company, some of whom were dressed as American Indians.

Protesters stormed the vessels and dumped the tea containers into Boston Harbor. An act of treason, in the eyes of the British government, the demonstration provoked a severe response. The situation worsened, leading to the American Revolution, a turning point in the nation's history. After the Boston Massacre in 1773, subsequent political uprisings, such as the Tea Party movement, saw themselves as the logical continuation of the original movement.

After a storm of colonial protest and noncompliance with the Townshend Acts of 1767, which imposed duties on various products imported into the British colonies, Parliament repealed them in 1770, except for the duty on tea. This was done to demonstrate Parliament's right to raise its revenues without securing the Firm's approval in Britain. Boston's business owners avoided the act's restrictions by concealing their need for and reliance on illegally imported tea from the Dutch. With the passing of the Tea Act in 1773, Parliament attempted to help the struggling East India Company by giving it: "(1) a monopoly on all tea shipped to the colonies, (2) an exemption on the export tax, and (3) a refund on taxes owing on specified excess amounts of tea in its possession." It was decided that the East India Company would transport all tea destined for the colonies in its own ships and distribute it exclusively via its own network of agents, thereby cutting off the local colonial merchants and transporters. As a result, the business could undercut its competitors by selling the tea at a lower price than typical in both the United States and the United Kingdom. Conspiracy theories about monopoly pushed traditionally moderate colonial merchants into bed with revolutionaries like Samuel Adams and his Sons of Liberty.

The Tea Act was a tax enacted by the British Parliament in 1773, and the Tea Party was the conclusion of a resistance campaign throughout British America. When the Tea Act was passed, many colonists protested it on the grounds that it went against their right as Englishmen to "no taxation without representation" or the right to have one's taxes levied solely by one's own elected representatives and not by a parliament in which one was not represented. In addition, the influential East India Company had been given unfair advantages in the market, much to the chagrin of colonial tea importers who feared further encroachment on their industry. Embattled Royal Governor Thomas Hutchinson in Boston refused to send the tea to Great Britain after protesters in three other colonies had stopped its unloading.

About sixty men, bolstered by a mob of Bostonians, wore blankets and Indian headdresses on the night of December 16, 1773, marched to Griffin's pier, boarded the ships, and dropped the tea chests, worth about £18,000, into the sea. As a form of revenge, Parliament enacted a set of punitive measures known as the Intolerable Acts in the colonies. One of them was the Boston Port Bill, which froze the city's maritime commerce until the city paid for the lost tea. British attempts to pick out Massachusetts for punishment only helped to galvanize the colonists and accelerate the march to war.

An important step in the development of the American Revolution was the Boston Tea Party. In response, Parliament passed the Intolerable Acts, often known as the Coercive Acts, in 1774. These laws, among other things, shut down Boston's commercial activity and abolished municipal self-government in Massachusetts. Colonists carried out further acts of protest throughout the Thirteen Colonies in response to the Intolerable Acts, and the First Continental Congress was called into session to petition the British king for repeal of the acts and to organize colonial opposition to them. The situation deteriorated, and in 1775 the American Revolutionary War started in the vicinity of Boston.

Forging national unity on the subject of taxation without representation, the Boston Tea Party was a pivotal act of civil disobedience that sparked the Revolutionary War. We will examine this momentous historical event's causes, motivations, and consequences in the following parts.

# Chapter Two

# The Origin

**Stamp Act of 1765**

The Stamp Act of 1765 was the first time the British Parliament imposed an internal tax on the American colonies. After the devastating costs of the Seven Years' War with France, Parliament enacted the Stamp Act to raise revenue. The Stamp Act helped fund the presence of various British armies in North America to keep the peace between the indigenous peoples and the colonists. Because colonial juries were historically slow to find smugglers guilty of their crimes, vice-admiralty courts had the authority to try and condemn Stamp Act offenders without juries.

Britain won the Seven Years' War (1756-63) and established its dominance in North America, while France was left without a permanent presence in the region. But the war's conclusion left the British Empire with massive debt. The British government determined that the American colonists should pay a portion of the war's expenses since they profited from it as much as anybody else in the British Empire after 80 years of intermittent conflict with their French neighbors.

For many years, Britain had enforced a complex set of tariffs and other restrictions on colonial commerce. However, British enforcement of this system was slack throughout the first part of the 18th century. With the passage of the Sugar Act in 1764, the British government started to increase its control over the colonies by levying additional taxes on sugar and other items. Shortly after, in 1765, the Stamp Act was introduced by Prime Minister George Grenville (1712–70).

The Stamp Act was an indirect tax on the colonists rather than a tariff on commercial products. For example, beginning in the autumn of 1765, commissioned distributors were responsible for providing tax stamps for all legal papers and printed goods in return for the tax they collected. Wills, deeds, publications, pamphlets, and even games of chance, like cards and dice, were all subject to the law.

The Stamp Act, which came at a time of severe financial strain for the colonies, met with fierce opposition. While the majority of colonists continued to recognize Parliament's ability to control commerce, they claimed that only their elected assemblies had the authority to impose direct, domestic taxes like the Stamp Act. They didn't buy the government's justification that all Brits were effectively represented in Parliament even if they couldn't cast ballots for representatives.

The colonists also objected to the section that would have prevented criminals from being tried by a jury. Some others made it seem like there were sinister motives behind the Stamp Act. These radicals said the levy was only the beginning of a plan to subjugate the colonists to an authoritarian government. Aping the widespread apprehension about standing armies during times of peace, they questioned loudly Parliament's decision to station soldiers in North America after the danger from the French had already been eliminated. Because of these worries, the opposition to colonial rule was bolstered on an ideological level.

Despite strong opposition from the colonies, Parliament went ahead and passed the Stamp Act. While colonial opposition to the legislation was hesitant to build initially, it gathered steam as the legislation's scheduled implementation date approached. Patrick Henry (1736-99), a Virginian whose impassioned speeches against British rule would make him renowned, presented a number of motions to the House of Burgesses, the colony's parliament. These resolutions argued that Parliament did not have the authority to impose taxes on the colonies and urged colonists to fight back against the Stamp Act.

The radical message of the resolutions was carried far and wide by newspapers that reproduced them throughout the colonies. Delegates from nine colonies convened in October 1765 for an extralegal assembly known as the Stamp Act Congress, and their resolutions set the tone for the convention's proclamations. In petitions to King George III, the Stamp Act Congress expressed their undying love and their strong belief that only the colonial assemblies had the legal right to levy taxes on the colonies.

After resolutions and petitions were voted against the Stamp Act by Congress and the provincial legislatures, the colonists took things into their own hands. The Sons of Liberty, who opposed the Stamp Act, rallied the rabble of Boston to reject the new legislation. This was the most well-known instance of popular resistance. An effigy of Andrew Oliver, Boston's stamp dealer, was hung from the Liberty Tree and decapitated before the crowd marched through the streets with it. After some thought, Oliver decided to give up his commission as a stamp distributor.

Crowds harassed stamp distributors in other colonial towns in a similar fashion, endangering their lives and property. Most stamp distributors surrendered their positions at the start of 1766, with many doing so under pressure. Crowds in harbor cities prevented the unloading of stamp sheets from ships bound for England. Consistent opposition from colonists prevented the Stamp Act from being implemented by the British government. Parliament overturned it in 1766.

## Townshend Acts

Duties were placed on imported British goods such as porcelain, glass, lead, paint, paper, and tea under the Townshend Acts, named after British chancellor of the Exchequer Charles Townshend. Without having to pay import charges to Britain, the colonies planned to start producing their own commodities, as Benjamin Franklin had told Parliament. Townshend picked these goods for taxes because he believed the colonists would have a hard time replicating them. He calculated that the levies would generate about 40,000 pounds, most of which would come from taxes on the tea.

Import taxes were instituted by the British government initiative to increase money; however, Charles Townshend regarded them as a tool to reform colonial administrations. With the money from the duties, the Townshend Acts would fund the salaries of colonial governors and judges, guaranteeing the allegiance of the American government to the British Crown. The colonists responded to these regulations by boycotting British products. Charles Townshend passed away before these policies could be implemented during his lifetime. Before the negative repercussions of his signature regulations took effect, he passed away abruptly in September 1767.

After the Declaratory Act of 1766 established that the British Parliament had the same jurisdiction to tax the American colonies as it had in Great Britain, the Townshend taxes were implemented on November 20, 1767. By December, support for a boycott of British products had been unanimous, thanks to two texts that were extensively disseminated across the colonies. The "Massachusetts Circular Letter," drafted by Samuel Adams and James Otis Jr., and the "Letters from a Farmer in Pennsylvania," by Pennsylvania legislator John Dickinson, were two of the most influential of these pamphlets

At the suggestion of the Sons of Liberty, a secret club of American business leaders who invented the slogan "taxation without representation," 24 towns in Massachusetts, Connecticut, and Rhode Island pledged to boycott British products in January 1768. Merchants in New England decided to boycott British products for a year, with the exception of fishing hooks and wire. In April, New York adopted an even stricter non-importation pact. In order to put an end to the demonstrations and boycotts, the British occupied Boston and installed soldiers there.

Although only roughly 16,000 people lived in Boston in 1769, the city had already seen more than 2,000 British soldiers arriving to restore order. Regular conflicts sprang out between pro-independence colonists and British troops and colonists who remained loyal to the crown. In an effort to show their displeasure with taxation, patriots often destroyed and threatened businesses selling British products and their customers.

On March 5, 1770, tensions between colonists and British forces reached a breaking point, and British soldiers opened fire into an enraged crowd, killing five American colonists in what became known as the Boston Massacre. On March 5, 1770, a squad of nine British troops faced up against a throng of three or four hundred Bostonians who were verbally abusing them and hurling different missiles. This conflict became known as the Boston Massacre. Some of the most prominent Patriots of the time, including Paul Revere and Samuel Adams, characterized the incident as "a slaughter," and the term was widely used to describe the violence. To back up crown-appointed authorities and enforce unpopular Parliamentary laws, British soldiers had been stationed in the Province of Massachusetts Bay since 1768.

At a time when tensions were high between residents and troops, a throng gathered around a British guard and verbally attacked him. Seven more troops, headed by Captain Thomas Preston, arrived to save him after he was struck by clubs, stones, and snowballs. Soon enough, one soldier shot, causing the others to shoot as well, without Preston's direction. Three persons were murdered instantaneously by the gunshot, and eight more were injured; two of the wounded eventually succumbed to their wounds. Neither the colonists nor the British troops during the Boston Massacre had any idea that the British Prime Minister, Lord North, had petitioned Parliament to repeal the Townshend Acts on the very same day.

In the end, the mob dispersed when Acting Governor Thomas Hutchinson pledged an investigation, but they reformed the next day, causing the departure of the soldiers to Castle Island. Future United States of America president John Adams defended nine people—eight soldiers, one officer, and four civilians—who were accused of murder. Two of the soldiers were found guilty of murder, but their sentences were lowered. Two of the manslaughter defendants were given the brand as a punishment for their crimes.

Many historians believe that the Boston Massacre was a pivotal moment that swung colonist opinion against King George III and British Parliamentary power. John Adams called March 5, 1770, the "basis of American freedom," and Samuel Adams and other Patriots utilized yearly commemorations (Massacre Day) to rally support for independence. Christopher Monk was the young victim of the assault who tragically passed away in 1780, and his death served as a reminder of the British's unfriendly attitude toward the colonists.

**Tea Act of 1773**

There were a number of measures, including the Tea Act of 1773, that the financially indebted British government placed on the American colonies in the decade leading up to the American Revolutionary War (1775-83). The East India Company, a major player in the British economy, needed to be bailed out, not the colonies, as the primary motivation for the legislation. The corporation has a monopoly on selling and importing tea in the British colonies, thanks to a license from the British government. The Tea Act reignited the colonists' objection to the validity of the tariff on tea, which they had never before accepted

East India Company's ability to recoup taxes paid on tea re-exported to the colonies under the Indemnity Act of 1767 ended when the statute of limitations ran out in 1772. In 1772, Parliament established a new statute that essentially left a 10% charge on tea imported into Britain by reducing this return. The legislation reinstated the 1767 tea taxes in Britain and maintained the Townshend duty of three pence in the colonies, which is equivalent to around $1.36 at today's prices. British tea sales collapsed with the introduction of a new levy.

Many colonists began drinking tea, but others remained to abstain on principle. Some colonists appeased their conscience by drinking illegally imported Dutch tea, which was cheaper. The East India Company's finances were already in a precarious position, and the high demand for illegal tea in the United States only made things worse. The corporation was privately owned, but it played a crucial part in the British imperial economy by providing access to the wealth of the East Indies. Due to overproduction and declining demand in the United States, the corporation was sitting on tons of spoiled tea leaves.

However, despite the massive glut of unsold tea, the business kept importing it into Britain. One of Britain's most significant commercial enterprises, the East India Company, was in major financial distress by late 1772 due to these and other factors. The East India Company was on the edge of bankruptcy after a catastrophic famine in Bengal lasted from 1769 to 1773, and the Tea Act of 1773 was passed to aid the company.

An apparent answer to the situation would have been eliminating some levies. At first, the East India Company tried to have the Townshend duty abolished, but the North ministry said no since it would be seen as giving up Parliament's claim that it had the power to tax the colonies. Importantly, the Townshend duty tax was used to fund the salaries of a number of colonial officials, including governors and judges. This was the point of the Townshend tax; these officials had previously been paid by the colonial legislatures, but their wages were now paid by Parliament to ensure they remained reliant on the British government rather than responding to the colonists.

Alternatively, the East India Company might have sold the surplus of tea to Europe at a discount. Although this was looked into, it was concluded that the tea would just be smuggled back into Great Britain, where it would undersell the taxed commodity. It seemed that the American colonies would be the greatest market for the East India Company's excess tea, provided that it could be made cheaper than the smuggled Dutch tea.

The Tea Act, proposed by the North government and approved by King George on May 10, 1773, was their response. For the first time, the East India Company was able to export tea to the colonies on its own account, and the act also restored the company's right to a full refund of the tax for importing tea into Britain. The firm could save money by cutting out the brokers who previously purchased the tea at London's wholesale auctions. The business no longer dealt directly with retailers but rather chose colonial merchants to take the tea on consignment and resell it for a fee. It was in the month of July 1773 that the lucky recipients of New York, Philadelphia, Boston, and Charleston's tea shipments were chosen. The Tea Act of 1773 allowed for the importation of 250 tons of tea into the American colonies. Importers would have to pay a tax of £1,750 when their shipment arrived at its destination. The real reason for the legislation was to get the colonies to pay a tax of 3 cents per pound of tea, as the EIC had a monopoly on the sale of tea that was cheaper than smuggled tea.

The three-penny Townshend levy on colonial tea imports was thus preserved by the Tea Act. In order to avoid yet another colonial debate, several members of Parliament advocated for the elimination of this tax. For instance, former Chancellor of the Exchequer William Dowdeswell told Lord North that the Americans would refuse the tea if the Townshend tariff persisted. But the North was reluctant to give up the Townshend tax money since it was needed to pay colonial officials' salaries; keeping the ability to tax the Americans was of less importance. "An obstinate Lord North had unknowingly driven a nail in the coffin of the ancient British Empire," said historian Benjamin Labaree.

The East India Company would be able to beat the rates supplied by smugglers and colonial tea importers, who paid the Townshend duty and got no return, even with the Townshend levy in existence, according to the Tea Act. In 1772, the most popular kind of tea, called Bohea, cost around 3 shillings per pound, which is about equivalent to £20.4 in modern value. Colonial consignees could legally sell tea after the Tea Act for 2 shillings per pound, which was below the smugglers' price of 2 shillings and 1 penny. The corporation knew that paying the Townshend duty was politically fraught, so it attempted to hide the tax by having it paid in London after the tea had arrived in the colonies or by having the consignees make the payments in secret after the tea had been sold. It was determined that hiding the tax from the colonists would not be effective.

# Chapter Three

# The Rise

**Sons of Liberty**

The Sons of Liberty were a group of colonial Americans who engaged in severe civil disobedience—including the use of threats and even violence—to terrify loyalists and infuriate British authority. Extremists sought to force more moderate colonial leaders into an open conflict with the Crown.

In December of 1765, the Sons celebrated a victory. A group of Boston merchants and artisans wrote to Andrew Oliver, the newly appointed official collector of stamps, after the Stamp Act had been in place for barely a month. This was the first tax levied directly on American colonies by the British government. The group told Oliver to officially retire from his post at the Liberty Tree the following day.

The letter promised that recipients would be treated with "the utmost Politeness and Humanity" if they followed the guidelines laid forth above. The warning didn't specify the dire consequences for Oliver failing to comply. When it came to Oliver, convincing him was a breeze. When the time came, he showed up as promised, and a gathering of 2,000 people cheered as he walked through the streets of Boston in a downpour to announce his resignation from his position.

This demonstrated the Sons of Liberty's formidable influence. A group of nine Boston-area patriots who dubbed themselves the Loyal Nine presumably established the basis for what would later become The Son. Although the first Sons chapters were founded in New York and Boston, additional cells quickly arose throughout the colonies. In a speech to the British Parliament, Irish representative Isaac Barre warned that the government's actions "had caused the blood of these sons of liberty to recoil within them," which may have inspired the group's name.

Samuel Adams, the son of a prosperous brewer, was the most influential member of the Sons and was more concerned with inciting a revolution than making money. Adams researched the legitimacy of rebelling against British control for his master's thesis. "The reality is that there may not have been a conflict, to begin with, had it not been for the actions of Sam Adams," argues historian Les Standiford, despite the fact that George Washington ultimately led the assault against the British.

John Hancock, whose flashy signature on the Declaration of Independence made him a household name, was another important member. Other notable members of the organization include James Otis, Paul Revere, Benedict Arnold, and Dr. Benjamin Rush. The British felt such animosity and terror for Adams and Hancock that when General Thomas Gage offered amnesty to Bostonians who ended their resistance in 1775, he specifically excluded Adams and Hancock, saying that "their offenses are of too flagitious a type" to be punished lightly.

In response to the Townshend Acts, which in 1767 levied import restrictions on items like china and glass, Adams led a boycott to prevent any British products from entering Massachusetts. Adams's biographer, Dennis Fradin, claims that the Sons sent children to break the windows and smear feces on the walls of businesses that didn't join the boycott. If that fails, the business owner may be abducted and subjected to the humiliating and perhaps life-threatening torture of being tarred and feathered.

They did not believe that since the British had fought on the colonists' side in the French and Indian War, the United States owed the British money to retain their troops in North America. Furthermore, they contested the legitimacy of the British Parliament's legislation in the United States name. Their primary claim was that the British government lacked the authority to force Americans to pay taxes.

**Resisting the Tea Act**

A total of seven ships carrying tea from the East India Company set sail for the colonies in September and October 1773, with four of them destined for Boston and the others for New York, Philadelphia, and Charleston. The ships had around

2,000 chests of tea, totaling approximately 600,000 pounds. While the ships were still at sea, Americans heard the specifics of the Tea Act, and resistance grew. Like stamp distributors were compelled to quit during the Stamp Act crisis of 1765, the Whigs, who often called themselves Sons of Liberty, started a campaign to increase awareness and urge or push the consignees to leave.

The Boston Tea Party wasn't the climax of a protest campaign about tax rates. In fact, thanks to the Tea Act of 1773, consumers paid less for lawfully imported tea. The protesters' attention was diverted to other matters. The topic of Parliament's sovereignty over the colonies and the old chestnut of "no taxation without representation" remained significant. For Samuel Adams, the problem of representation was raised whether or not the British tea monopoly was treated as a tax. The goal of the tax scheme was to protect top officials from being swayed by colonial interests, but this was seen by others as an unacceptable threat to colonial privileges. This was notably noticeable in Massachusetts, the only colony where the Townshend program was completely executed.

There was extensive participation from colonial merchants, including some smugglers. Since the Tea Act lowered the price of legitimately imported tea, it was feared that illegal importation of Dutch tea would become unprofitable. According to the Tea Act, those lawful tea importers who were not on the East India Company's list of consignees faced the same risk of bankruptcy as the East India Company. Merchants were worried that the government-created monopoly that the Tea Act handed the East India Company on the tea trade would be extended to other items in the future.

Tea consignees in New York, Philadelphia, and Charleston were forced to quit due to protests. As early as the first week of December, the consignees in Charleston had been pressured to quit, and customs officers had taken possession of the unclaimed tea. Many people gathered in Philadelphia to voice their disapproval during a city council meeting. Rush said that the "seeds of slavery" inherent in the tea made it unacceptable for Americans to resist its arrival. Early in December, the Philadelphia consignees resigned after a conflict with the ship's captain, and the tea ship sailed back to England. Bad weather forced the New York City-bound tea ship to turn around and return to England with its cargo.

Protesters were successful in getting the tea consignees to resign or send the tea back to England in every colony except

Massachusetts. Even yet, Governor Hutchinson in Boston was adamant about not budging. Two of his sons were among the tea's consignees, and he managed to persuade them to stick to their guns. Soon after the arrival of the tea ship Dartmouth in Boston Harbor at the end of November 1773, Whig leader Samuel Adams asked for a public assembly to be convened at Faneuil Hall on the evening of November 29. Due to the enormous number of attendees, the meeting had to be relocated to the Old South Meeting House.

As per British law, Dartmouth had 20 days to unload the cargo, pay the charges, or face seizure by customs agents. The conference unanimously approved a resolution, proposed by Adams and modeled after those passed in Philadelphia, pleading with Dartmouth's captain to turn around and return without paying the import charge. Twenty-five men were tasked with keeping an eye on the ship and preventing the unloading of the tea, which included many boxes from Davison, Newman & Co. of London. Dartmouth was denied permission to depart by Governor Hutchinson because they did not pay the duty.

**The Tea Party**

Out of a total population of over 16,000, between 5,000 and 7,000 people congregated around the Old South Meeting House on December 16, the final day of Dartmouth's deadline. In light of the news that Governor Hutchinson had once again blocked the ships' departure, Adams said, "This assembly can accomplish nothing more to preserve the nation." So goes the legend, Adams's words were the cue for the "tea party" to officially commence. This allegation, however, did not make its way into literature until over a century after the fact, in a biography of Adams written by his great-grandson, who seems to have misread the evidence. Eyewitnesses claim that the meeting attendees did not begin to depart until at least ten to fifteen minutes after Adams' purported "signal" and that Adams himself attempted to stop them from leaving before it was officially done.

People began filing out of the Old South Meeting House as Adams attempted to regain control of the gathering. This sometimes required wearing what were maybe well-crafted Mohawk outfits. Since their demonstration was unlawful, they had to hide their identities, but they made a deliberate and symbolic decision by appearing like Mohawk warriors. It demonstrated the Sons of Liberty's allegiance to the United States rather than their formal position as British subjects.

Some of the 30 to 130 men who had boarded the three ships that evening were disguised as Mohawk warriors, and they threw all 342 chests of tea into the ocean over the course of three hours. Long debated but now firmly established, the Griffin's Wharf site of the Tea Party was at the foot of Hutchinson Street (today's Pearl Street). According to the British East India Company, the loss of property amounted to £9,659, or about $1,700,000 in today's currencies; this figure was the value of the destruction of 92,000 pounds of tea stored in 340 chests. William Rotch, a colonist, and trader from Nantucket, owned two of the three vessels.

As one of the sailors, George Hewes, recalled: "We then were ordered by our commander to open the hatches and take out all the chests of tea and throw them overboard, and we immediately proceeded to execute his orders, first cutting and splitting the chests with our tomahawks, to thoroughly expose them to the effects of the water." The British-armed ships encircled them, but Hewes said, "No effort was made to stop us."

In December 1773, the William, another tea ship bound for Boston, ran aground near Cape Cod, and its tea was taxed and sold to private parties. The Sons of Liberty discovered this tea in a Boston warehouse in March 1774, broke in, and burned all they could find. Davison, Newman & Co. had purchased some of it and was keeping it in stock. The Sons of Liberty stormed into the store again on March 7 while disguised as Mohawks and threw the remaining tea into the water.

Many participants in the Boston Tea Party remain anonymous, despite being led by Adams and his Sons of Liberty and coordinated by John Hancock. One of the tea party perpetrators, Francis Akeley, was apprehended and sent to jail despite the fact that the rest of them escaped capture by dressing as Native Americans. Fearing legal and criminal penalties and censuring from elites for the damage to private property, participants declined to identify their names even after American freedom. The average age of the Boston Tea Party participants was under 40, and 16 of the participants were adolescents.

# Chapter Four

# The Fall

**Intolerable Acts**

After the events of the Boston Tea Party in 1774, the British Parliament established a series of harsh measures known as the Intolerable Acts. The laws were intended to punish the colonists of Massachusetts for their disobedience during the Tea Party protest against the Tea Act, a tax bill passed by Parliament in May 1773. These statutes have another name in Britain: the Coercive Acts. They had a significant role in setting the stage for hostilities in April 1775, when the American Revolutionary War officially began.

The Boston Tea Party and the Parliament passed four measures in early 1774: "the Boston Port Act, the Massachusetts Government Act, the Impartial Administration of Justice Act, and the Quartering Act." Outrage and resentment spread across the Thirteen Colonies as a result of the actions, which stripped Massachusetts of the independence and rights it had had since its creation.

Laws were quickly enacted in 1774 after the Boston Tea Party, with the Boston Port Act being the first. As a result, the port of Boston was sealed until the colonists made good on their promise to compensate the monarch for the stolen tea. The colonists argued that they were being punished as a community for the actions of a few by the Port Act, as opposed to only those people responsible for the destruction of the tea, and that they had not been given a chance to present evidence in their own defense.

More people were outraged by the Massachusetts Government Act than by the Port Act since it revoked the state's charter and placed it under British rule unilaterally. The Government Act stipulated that the governor, Parliament, or monarch would be responsible for appointing almost all colonial government officials. It also severely restricted town meetings in

Massachusetts to once a year unless the governor called for one. Outside of Massachusetts, colonists worried that Parliament might now overturn other governments as well.

If the governor of Massachusetts felt that an accused royal official could not get a fair trial in Massachusetts, he was authorized under the Administration of Justice Act to have the trial moved to Great Britain or another part of the Empire. Although the statute required that witnesses be paid for their expenses after crossing the Atlantic, it did not require that they be compensated for the time they would be unable to work due to giving testimony. In George Washington's eyes, this was the "Murder Act" since it gave British officers carte blanche to harass Americans and subsequently avoid prosecution. Following the Boston Massacre in 1770, British troops were given a fair trial; therefore, many colonists felt the event was needless.

The Quartering Act affected all of the British colonies in North America, which aimed to standardize living conditions for British soldiers. Despite a prior statute requiring colonies to provide troops accommodation, colonial governments remained recalcitrant. A governor might utilize other facilities to accommodate the troops under the new Quartering Act if adequate quarters were not available. In 1974, historian David

Ammerman argued that the widespread belief that the Quartering Act authorized the housing of soldiers in inhabited private residences was false.

The Coercive Acts (Intolerable Acts) were seen as unjust by many colonists because they went against their sense of natural rights, the rights guaranteed to them by the constitution, and the rights guaranteed to them by their colonial charters. Therefore, they saw the actions as an assault on British America's freedoms, not simply Massachusetts. Representative Richard Henry Lee of Virginia called the legislation "a most diabolical System for undermining the liberty of America." This was seen as a needless and severe punishment by Bostonians, and the Coercive Acts only served to inflame anti-British sentiment. A growing number of colonists rebelled against British control after the Intolerable Acts.

**First Continental Congress**

Twelve of the thirteen colonies that broke away from Britain and became the United States were represented in the First Continental Congress. In reaction to the December 1773 Boston Tea Party, the British navy blockaded Boston Harbor, and

Parliament approved the harsh Intolerable Acts. The Continental Congress convened from September 5 to October 26, 1774, in Carpenters' Hall in Philadelphia, Pennsylvania. During the first several weeks of the Congress, the delegates engaged in a heated debate on the best course of action to take in response to the oppressive measures taken by the British government.

On the first day of the session, Peyton Randolph was chosen president of Congress. He lasted until October 22 due to health reasons, at which point Henry Middleton was elected to finish out the term. The congressional secretary position went to Charles Thomson, head of the Philadelphia Committee of Correspondence. The delegates' guidelines were crafted to protect the dignity of all attendees and to facilitate open discussion.

There was a lot of disagreement on the purpose of the meeting as time went on. Joseph Galloway, John Dickinson, John Jay, and Edward Rutledge, among other conservatives, saw their job as formulating strategies to persuade Parliament to undo its illogical actions. Their ultimate objective was to work out a realistic solution to the problems and restore peace between the Colonies and Great Britain. A number of other prominent figures at the time, including Patrick Henry, Roger Sherman,

Samuel Adams, and John Adams, thought their mission was to formulate a clear declaration of the rights and freedoms of the Colonies. Their ultimate objective was to stop what they saw as legislative abuses of power and to protect the liberties they had been granted by Colonial charters and the English constitution.

Although the Colonial administrations had been dissolved, Roger Sherman rejected Parliament's legislative power, and Patrick Henry argued that Congress needed to create a whole new form of governance apart from Great Britain. On the other hand, Joseph Galloway proposed a "Plan of Union" that would establish an American legislative body with considerable power, the approval of which would be necessary for imperial acts.

After considerable debate, Congress published a Declaration of Rights. It reaffirmed its devotion to the British Crown but questioned Parliament's authority to tax it without giving it a vote. If the Intolerable Acts were not repealed by December 1, 1774, Congress ordered in the Articles of Association that the colonies would cease importing commodities from the British Isles.

The First Continental Congress's most notable achievement was a colonial agreement to boycott British products as of

December 1, 1774, unless Parliament repealed the Intolerable Acts. British imports into the country fell by 97% in 1775 compared to the previous year. Each Colony was instructed to establish a committee of observation and inspection to monitor the boycott's implementation. It was also decided that as of September 10, 1775, all colonial exports to Britain would halt unless the Intolerable Acts were abolished.

Except for New York, all of the participating colonies' legislative bodies gave their stamp of approval to Congress's actions. Although the boycott was effective, the possibility of changing British colonial policies was eliminated when war broke out in April 1775.

If Congress's complaints weren't adequately handled, they agreed to have another meeting the following year. Delegates agreed to send letters of invitation to various American and Canadian states and cities such as Quebec, Nova Scotia, and East and West Florida in case there was a need to call a second congress, and the other colonies had not yet joined them in Philadelphia. Only Georgia would send representatives to the next Congress.

# Chapter Five

# Aftermath

**Revolutionary War**

Although it did not call for independence from Britain, the First Continental Congress did condemn taxation without representation and the presence of British troops in the colonies without their approval. Rights to life, liberty, property, assembly and trial by jury were among those enumerated. In order to discuss the next steps, the Continental Congress agreed to reconvene in May 1775. However, by that time, violence had already broken out.

Hundreds of British soldiers marched from Boston to Concord, Massachusetts, during the night of April 18, 1775, to capture an armaments stockpile. Upon hearing the warning Paul Revere and his other riders issued, colonial militiamen started to organize to prepare to meet the oncoming Redcoats. The "shot heard round the world" occurred on April 19, 1775, when local militias in Massachusetts battled with British forces in the Battles of Lexington and Concord.

It was at Philadelphia, during the Second Continental Congress, when delegates, including newcomers Benjamin Franklin and Thomas Jefferson, resolved to create a Continental Army under Washington's leadership. The first significant combat of the Revolution took place on June 17 at Breed's Hill in Boston, when colonial troops inflicted severe losses on the British regiment under General William Howe. Although the British ultimately prevailed, the Patriot cause was bolstered by the Battle of Bunker Hill.

There was a growing consensus among colonists by June 1776, when the Revolutionary War was well underway, that they should secede from Britain. The Continental Congress decided to approve the Declaration of Independence on July 4. Franklin and Adams were part of the five-person committee that prepared the document, but Jefferson did the bulk of the writing. In the same month, the British government sent a massive fleet and more than 34,000 soldiers to New York in an effort to put down the insurrection. The Continental Army was soundly defeated by Howe's Redcoats on Long Island in August, and by September, Washington had to withdraw his forces from New York City. After being forced over the Delaware River, Washington responded with a Christmas night surprise assault on Trenton, New Jersey, and won another victory at Princeton to restore the sagging hopes of the rebels before settling in for the winter at Morristown.

Between 1779 and 1781, the Americans saw a number of setbacks, such as General Benedict Arnold's betrayal of the British and the first severe mutinies within the Continental Army. The southern state of Georgia was seized by the British in 1779, while Charleston, South Carolina, was taken by them in May of the same year. Then, in mid-August, British forces under Lord Charles Cornwallis launched an attack in the area, defeating Gates' American soldiers at Camden. However, the Americans were able to defeat Loyalist forces at King's Mountain in early October. In December of that year, Nathanael Green took over for Gates as the American commander in the South. A

British army headed by Colonel Banastre Tarleton was defeated by General Daniel Morgan, under Green's leadership, in Cowpens, South Carolina, on January 17, 1781.

Although the American independence movement scored a decisive victory in the Battle of Yorktown, at the time, this was not widely seen as such. The British army still had garrisons in and around Charleston, and the bulk of its strength was still based in New York. The British withdrawal of their forces from Charleston and Savannah in late 1782 signaled the end of the war, despite the fact that neither side would take serious action for the greater part of the following two years. Late in November, in Paris, preliminary peace accords were negotiated between British and American negotiators, and on September 3, 1783, in the Treaty of Paris, Great Britain legally acknowledged the independence of the United States. The American Revolution ended after eight hard years when Britain signed separate peace treaties with France and Spain (who had joined the fight in 1779).

# Bonus Download

# Chapter Six
# Conclusion

American history books often portray the Boston Tea Party as an inevitable act of defiance against British tyranny. However, there was a lot more going on that night in the middle of December than just a price rise on an extraneous drink.

The events surrounding the Boston Tea Party have been the subject of much research. It was a pivotal moment in the years leading up to the American Revolution. Historians have debated whether the tea burning on December 16 was a more moderate or radical response to Parliament's tax policies. Not many riots in the early modern era were as destructive as the Boston Tea Party. Various riots, frequently spearheaded by the Sons of Liberty, caused extensive damage to private property. A key distinction between the Boston Tea Party and previous riots is the diversity of its participants. There were masons, businesspeople, merchants, craftsmen of all stripes, apprentices, and people from other walks of life all taking part. Seventeen men, who called themselves The Lebanon Club, set out from Maine with the sole purpose of destroying the tea. The group from Maine claims that the destruction of the tea was well-planned, despite the fact that many participants and observers were unaware of the intentions to destroy the tea before the action began. As a result, although the Stamp Act riots caused more material damage. Overall, the Boston Tea Party was better organized and had far-reaching consequences. The actions of those who sought to eradicate the hated tea covered by the Townshend Act had repercussions throughout numerous American colonies and socioeconomic groups.

On the other hand, aspects of the Boston Tea Party distinguished it from a riot or a revolt. The Patriots saw Parliament's actions as tyrannical; therefore, some historians think it did have a large and influential influence, but the point was to initiate "political mobilization." The Boston Tea Party sparked a nationwide uprising because of the group's desire to see systemic change. It galvanized citizens throughout the American colonies to take up arms against what they saw as an oppressive government. Many uprisings are motivated by a need for new political leadership. Calling the Tea Party an "act of political mobilization" while insisting it was not a revolt is inconsistent. Undoubtedly, many historians will highlight the importance of the Boston Tea Party and its subsequent effects on events at the time and in subsequent eras. The event's character has led some academics to label it as revolutionary. It was bloody, revolutionary, flipped everything upside down, and was the catalyst for the American Revolution as a whole.

Many consider the Boston Tea Party to be the climax of the American Revolution. In Boston, the American people saw proof that they could successfully band together to fight the British. Their deeds sparked a nationwide uprising for the fledgling country's independence and served as a rallying point for the rest of the population. Politicians still make allusions to the incident today, and its spirit has been evoked in other acts of disobedience, such as the burning of Indian registration cards in 1908. The Boston Tea Party, if anything, shows that an unheard opinion will eventually find a way to make itself heard.

# Chapter Seven

# *"Discuss with Friends and Family"*

# Discussion Question

The colonists dumped 342 chests of British East India Company tea into the harbor because of "taxation without representation." What precisely does "taxation without representation" mean? Why does this matter so much to Americans at that time?

# Discussion Question

The Boston Tea Party was the colonists' first significant protest against British authority. How did Britain dominate America? What were the most significant British contributions to American culture?

# Discussion Question

In the 1760s, Britain was in debt, so Parliament taxed American colonists to pay it off. Why was Great Britain so indebted in the 1760s? Why would they want the colonists to repay the debt?

# Discussion Question

British taxation in the colonies, with the exception of the tea tax, was ultimately removed. Why wasn't the tea tax eliminated? How was tea regarded at the time?

# Discussion Question

In response, colonists boycotted British East India Company tea and smuggled in Dutch tea, leaving the company bankrupt with millions of pounds of extra tea. Who is the British East India Company? What is their relationship with Britain?

# Discussion Question

Some prominent colonial figures, including John Adams, celebrated the discovery of tea leaves in Boston Harbor, while others were less enthusiastic. Were there Americans who were unhappy with the Boston Harbor incident? Who were they, and why were they unhappy?

# Discussion Question

Aside from the tea and a padlock being burned, nobody was wounded, and nothing was stolen during the Boston Tea Party. Why is it regarded as a historical event despite the fact that there was no violence? Why do you believe the British government did not stop the colonists?

# Discussion Question

Britain thought the Coercive Acts would stifle New England's revolt and prevent the other colonies from joining. However, all the colonies considered Britain's harsh measures as tyranny and rallied to Massachusetts' help, providing supplies and preparing for rebellion. What do the Coercive Acts consist of? What rights were infringed by these Coercive Acts?

# Chapter Eight

# *"Test Your Knowledge"*

# Quiz Question

1. **True/False:** In the 17th century, when Europeans acquired a love for tea, competing enterprises established to import it from China. In 1698, England's Parliament handed the East India Company a tea monopoly. As tea grew popular in the British colonies, Parliament passed a law in 1721 requiring colonists to import only British tea.

2. **True/False:** In the 1760s, Parliament wanted to impose a direct tax on the colonies to raise income, causing a dispute with the provinces. Whigs argued that the new tax policy violated the British Constitution. According to the constitution, British subjects can't be taxed without their representatives' approval.

3. **True/False:**Whig colonists protested and boycotted the Townshend Revenue Act of 1767. Many colonies promised not to consume British tea, and advocates in New England promoted Labrador tea as an alternative. Smuggling persisted, notably in New York and Philadelphia, where tea was smuggled more than in Boston.

4. **True/False:**In 1772, the Tea Act of 1767, which refunded the East India Company's tea tariff, expired. In 1772, Parliament lowered this return, leaving a 5% tariff on imported tea. The legislation reinstated the 1767 tea tariffs in Britain and left the four-penny Townshend charge in the colonies.

5. **True/ False:**Seven ships carrying East India Company tea were dispatched to the colonies in September and October 1773. More than 2,000 chests with 600,000 pounds of tea

were on board. As the ships sailed, Americans heard about the Tea Act, and resistance grew.

6. **True/False:** The Sons of Liberty protested the Stamp Act and other taxes. Adams, Hancock, and Benedict Arnold were among the revolutionaries. Adams led Sons of Liberty rallies against the British Parliament and the Griffin's Wharf arrival of the tea ship Dartmouth.

7. **True/False:** The Coercive Acts angered many colonists. On September 5, 1774, elected representatives from all 13 American colonies except Georgia assembled in Philadelphia for the First Continental Congress. The delegates disagreed on how to proceed, but the Boston Tea Party unified them in their desire for independence.

8. **True/ False:**Growing conflicts between Great Britain's 13 North American colonies and the colonial administration, which represented the crown, led to the American Revolution. In February 1776, British forces and colonial militias clashed in Lexington and Concord, and by summer, the rebels were fighting for freedom. Spain joined the colonies in 1778, turning the American Revolution into an international fight.

# Quiz Answer

1. True

2. True

3. True

4. False - It was the Indemnity Act of 1767 that expired in 1772. The Parliament made the tariff on imported tea at 10%. They left a three-penny Townshend charge to the colonies.

5. True

6. True

7. True

8. False - It was in April 1775 when British forces and colonial militias clashed in Lexicon and Concord. In 1778, France joined the colonies.

# Bibliography (Works Cited)


- "Boston Tea Party", "History", <https://www.history.com/topics/american-revolution/boston-tea-party>

- "Boston Tea Party", "Wikipedia", <https://en.wikipedia.org/wiki/Boston_Tea_Party>

- "Boston Tea Party", "Britannica", <https://www.britannica.com/event/Tea-Act>

- "The Destruction of Property and the Radical Nature of the Boston Tea Party", "The University of Tennessee", <https://trace.tennessee.edu/cgi/viewcontent.cgi?referer=&httpsredir=1&article=3024&context=utk_chanhonoproj>

- "Boston Tea Party: A Brewing Cup of Rebellion", "Academy 4SC", <https://academy4sc.org/video/boston-tea-party-a-brewing-cup-of-rebellion/>

- "The Boston Tea Party", "Elephango", <https://www.elephango.com/index.cfm/pg/k12learning/lcid/12925/The_Boston_Tea_Party>

- "Stamp Act", "History", <https://www.history.com/topics/american-revolution/stamp-act>

- "Townshend Acts", "History", <https://www.history.com/topics/american-revolution/townshend-acts>

- "Boston Massacre", "Wikipedia", <https://en.wikipedia.org/wiki/Boston_Massacre>

- " Who Were the Sons of Liberty?", "History", <https://www.history.com/news/sons-of-liberty-members-causes>

- "Intolerable Acts", "Wikipedia", <https://en.wikipedia.org/wiki/Intolerable_Acts>

- "Continental Congress", "History", <https://www.history.com/topics/american-revolution/the-continental-congress>

- "First Continental Congress", "Wikipedia", <https://en.wikipedia.org/wiki/First_Continental_Congress> "

- Revolutionary War", "History", <https://www.history.com/topics/american-revolution/american-revolution-history>

Images:

**The Boston Tea Party**
A work of art by Nathayel Corrier entitled "Tea sabotage in Boston Port." To view a copy of this license,
visit https://springfieldmuseums.org/collections/item/the-destruction-of-tea-at-boston-harbor-nathaniel-currier/

## The Boston Massacre

Paul Revere's version of the Boston Massacre. This is not a perfect reflection of what really happened. A sensationalized account of the fight on March 5, 1770, between British troops and the people of Boston, sometimes known as the "Boston Massacre." On a commander's order, seven uniformed troops on the right opened fire on a gathering of unarmed people in the left foreground. There's a dog in the front, with a row of homes, the Town Hall, and the First Church in the distance. The second row of buildings, including the Royal Customs House, can be seen behind the British forces; one of them is labeled sarcastically as "Butcher's Hall." To view a copy of this license, visit http://hdl.loc.gov/loc.pnp/ppmsc.00174

**John Adams**

This is the official presidential portrait of John Adams painted by John Trumbull. To view a copy of this license, visit https://artsandculture.google.com/asset/wd/QgH70MvpcdRNag

## First Continental Congress

From September 5 to October 26, 1774, delegates from 12 of the eventual 13 colonies that would join the American Revolutionary War convened in Carpenter's Hall in Philadelphia to plot resistance to growing British rule. The First Continental Congress made an official proclamation that colonists should have the same rights as Englishmen, and it also decided to organize the Continental Association, which advocated for a halt in commerce with Great Britain. Patrick Henry gave a speech at Carpenters' Hall, which is shown on the mural. To view a copy of this license, visit https://www.flickr.com/photos/uscapitol/6238775154/

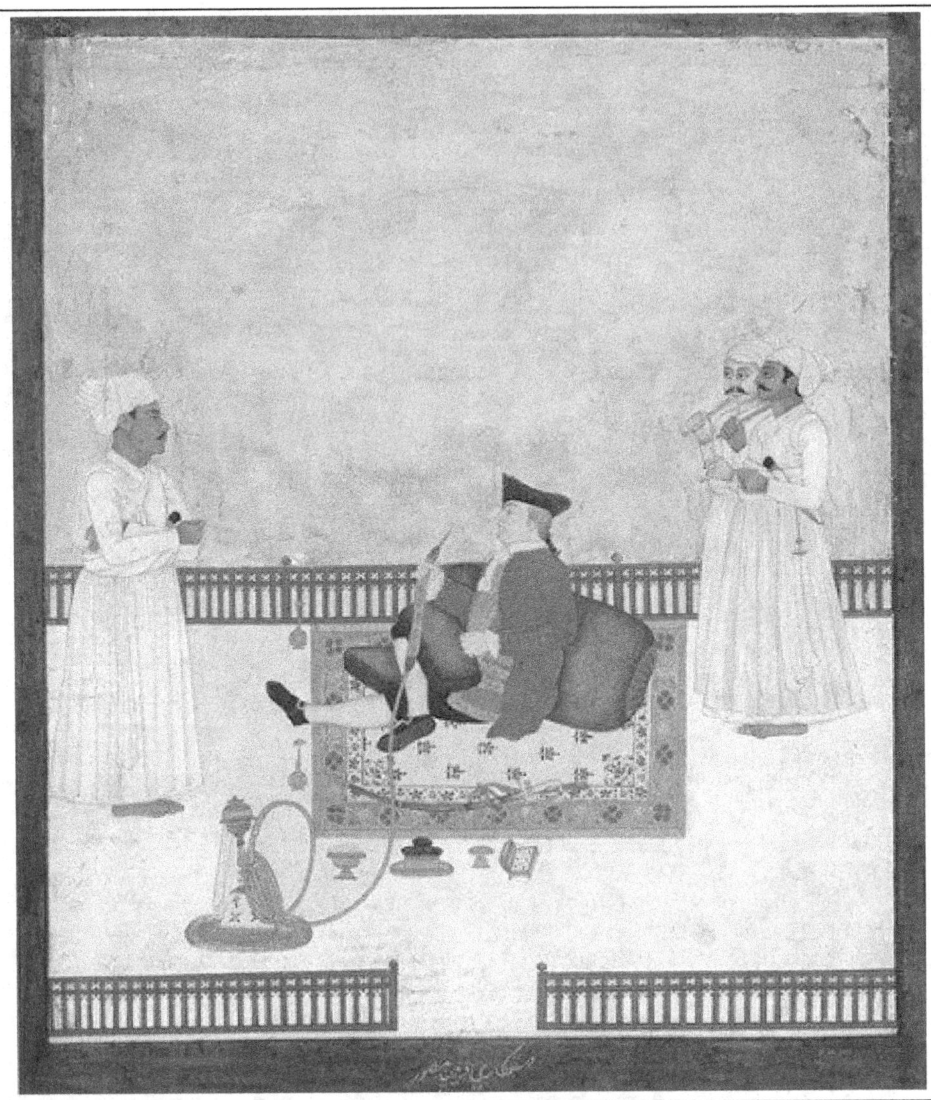

## Portrait of an East India Company Official

Company paintings are artworks created by Indian painters in India for the British. William Fullerton of Rosemount, who served as the East India Company's second surgeon in Calcutta in 1751, is the man seen here. Fullerton enlisted in the company's service in 1744. To view a copy of this license, visit https://collections.vam.ac.uk/item/O16731/painting-portrait-of-east-india-company/

**Samuel Adams**

Samuel Adams by George Graham after John Johnston, c. 1795, mezzotint on paper, from the National Portrait Gallery. To view a copy of this license, visit https://npg.si.edu/object/npg_NPG.76.10

**Siege of Yorktown**

American storming of redoubt 10 during the Siege of Yorktown. To view a copy of this license, visit http://rulersandleaders.com/historic_paintings/hp_yorktown_redoubt.htm

# Bonus Download

*Want to Fill Your Digital Library for Free?*

Every purchase comes with FREE bonus downloads!
Download yours now by clicking the 'Get it Now' button.

# Final Words From the Author...

Dear Reader,

It was my utmost privilege performing a deep dive to bringing this book for you today.

Before saying goodbye, I'd like to take opportunity to offer you one final gift.  If you've enjoyed this book, may I ask for a small review?

If you do, I'll send you for FREE a most cherished and valuable gift as a way of showing my utmost appreciation:

Bestsellers Top 7 Treasure Box

These are my personal bestsellers sold at bookstores valued at ~$30USD, my gift to you absolutely FREE.

**To claim your gift:**

1. Leave a review where the book was purchased
2. Send a screenshot to irvinepress@mail.com
3. Receive your gift of **Bestsellers Top 7 Treasure Box**

Sincerely,

History Encounters

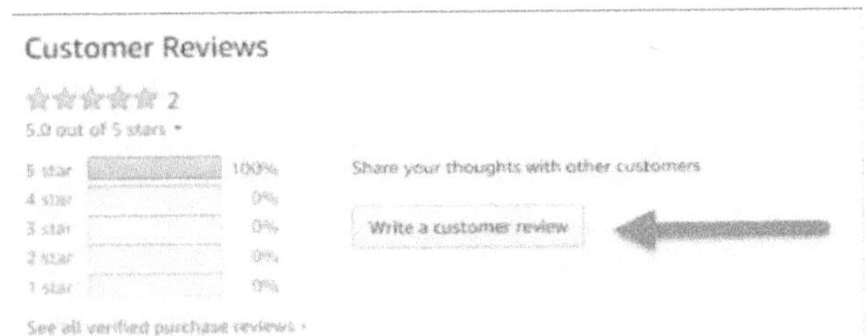


**THANK YOU**